GIN

and
Bear it

summersdale

An Hachette UK Company
www.hachette.co.uk

Summersdale Publishers Ltd
Part of Octopus Publishing Group Limited
Carmelite House
50 Victoria Embankment
LONDON
EC4Y 0DZ
UK

www.summersdale.com

Printed and bound in the Czech Republic

ISBN: 978-1-78685-200-7

Substantial discounts on bulk quantities of Summersdale books are available to corporations, professional associations and other organisations. For details contact general enquiries: telephone: +44 (0) 1243 771107 or email: enquiries@summersdale.com.

TO....................................

FROM..............................

DEFINITION OF GIN

Gin (mass noun): A clear alcoholic drink distilled from grain or malt and flavoured with juniper. London Dry Gin is the most popular, infused with botanicals during its second or third distillation process. Plymouth gin is similar, although it uses different aromatic ingredients and can only be produced in Plymouth. Old Tom Gin, the gin originally used in a Tom Collins, is a sweetened recipe that had almost fallen out of favour until the gin renaissance. Dutch or Genever gin is the original gin recipe, although it looks and tastes very different to the gin most people know and love today. Distilled from malt grains, it looks and tastes more like whiskey than other gins. Tonic's partner in crime (and fun!), and tasty in a number of cocktails. Perfect for all occasions, from a light tipple on a summer's day to long cosy evenings in dark bars.

A DASH OF HISTORY

Production of gin began in Holland in the early seventeenth century. It was first used as a medicinal drink to treat stomach aches, gout and gallstones. During the Thirty Years' War, gin made its way to the British troops fighting in the Low Countries. It was used to warm up (numb) the soldiers, who faced damp weather conditions, and also became the go-to when they needed a bit of Dutch courage.

Gin was slowly introduced to England upon the soldiers' return to their home country and distillation of the spirit commenced, albeit without any of the health and safety regulations that have to be adhered to nowadays.

It was the drink of choice for the poor and was blamed for crime, prostitution and mental illness until the Gin Act was introduced in September 1736, which put a tax on gin and introduced a licence for gin sellers. This provoked riots and made the spirit unaffordable to most, but only two distilleries agreed to the terms of the licence. Eight years later, the act was repealed and a new policy was drafted that set lower taxes, benefitting a bigger variety of good-quality distillers and retailers alike.

GIN FOR

If you haven't noticed already, gin is everywhere. In some pubs and restaurants they are even advertising it as a substitute for soup! In trendy bars, just take one glance and you'll notice hipsters supping the gin cocktail special while connoisseurs are testing the latest botanical flavours.

EVERYONE

Distilleries have been experimenting with new tastes and combinations to create exciting new gin flavours. Gin bars have also seen a rise in popularity, with mixologists recreating classic cocktails and inventing new and exclusive recipes of their own. With so many flavours to try, no wonder the gin boom has got everyone talking.

KNOWING YOUR BOTANICALS

There are many botanicals used in flavouring gin. Here are some of the most common ones:

Juniper – if a gin distillery doesn't use this coniferous plant in their production process then they can't promote their gin as distilled. It gives the gin a citrus taste, which can be enhanced with…

Lemon or orange peel – lemon and orange peel can be used together or separately in order to flavour gin. You can adjust the sweetness or bitterness of the flavour by changing the variety of orange you use.

Coriander – often considered the second most important botanical in gin, coriander seeds are used to add a touch of spice and fragrance to the mix.

Angelica root – another warming flavour and one of the nine traditional ingredients in gin-making.

Orris root – this is the bulb of the iris plant. It is bitter and takes up to four years to mature in preparation for use.

Liquorice, cassia bark and nutmeg – these, along with the previous six ingredients, comprise the nine traditional gin botanicals. Other modern, popular flavourings include ginger, cubeb berries, cardamom, almond, cinnamon, angelica seed and camomile flowers.

WHAT YOU NEED

In order to make the gin recipes in this book, you will find the following equipment useful.

A cocktail shaker – if you can find one that has a built-in strainer it will help you when you come to pour the cocktails. Alternatively, you can use a tea strainer.

A variety of different glasses – depending on the type of cocktail you are making, you will need an assortment of small and large glasses. Cocktail, old-fashioned, Collins, coupe, Sling, Martini and highball glasses and champagne flutes are the most commonly used.

Bar spoon – if you don't have one of these to hand, use chopsticks for when you need to stir a cocktail.

Lemon and lime squeezer – this is a useful piece of equipment to separate the pips from your freshly squeezed juice. Alternatively, you could use your hands and pick out the pips.

THE ONLY TIME
I EVER ENJOYED
IRONING WAS
THE DAY
I ACCIDENTALLY GOT

IN THE STEAM
IRON.

WHEN YOU STOP DRINKING,

YOU HAVE TO DEAL WITH THIS MARVELLOUS PERSONALITY THAT STARTED YOU DRINKING IN THE FIRST PLACE.

JIMMY BRESLIN

I'M NOT A HEAVY DRINKER; I CAN SOMETIMES GO FOR HOURS WITHOUT TOUCHING A DROP.

NOËL COWARD

GIN FIZZ

- 60 ml gin
- 1 tsp sugar or sugar syrup
- dash of freshly squeezed lemon juice
- soda water to finish
- slice of lemon to garnish
- 1 egg white (optional)

In a cocktail shaker filled with ice, mix together the gin, lemon juice, sugar or syrup and egg white. Shake vigorously and strain into a highball glass.

Fill to the top with soda water and serve with a slice of lemon.

Invented in the Imperial Cabinet Saloon, New Orleans in 1888 by Henry C. Ramos, this is a long-standing classic and New Orleans favourite.

I THINK THAT I WILL TAKE TWO SMALL BOTTLES OF DUBONNET AND GIN WITH ME THIS MORNING, IN CASE IT IS NEEDED.

THE QUEEN MOTHER

WHEn LIFE HAnDs YOu LEMQnS, OPEN THE GIN.

I'M A DRINKER
WITH WRITING
PROBLEMS.

BRENDAN BEHAN

WHEN YOU'RE

THIRSTY AND IT SEEMS THAT
YOU COULD DRINK THE ENTIRE
OCEAN, THAT'S FAITH; WHEN
YOU START TO DRINK AND
FINISH ONLY A GLASS OR
TWO, THAT'S SCIENCE.

ANTON CHEKHOV

BRAMBLE

- 60 ml gin
- 30 ml freshly squeezed lemon juice
- 15 ml sugar syrup
- 15 ml crème de mure
- blackberries to garnish

Fill an old-fashioned glass with crushed ice and add the gin, lemon juice and sugar syrup.

Top with more crushed ice and pour the crème de mure over the top. Garnish with a couple of blackberries.

Dick Bradsell, the legendary London bartender and inventor of the Bramble, also created other classics such as the Espresso Martini and Russian Spring Punch.

I EXERCISE STRONG SELF-CONTROL. I NEVER DRINK ANYTHING STRONGER THAN GIN BEFORE BREAKFAST.

W. C. FIELDS

IGNORANCE IS A LOT
LIKE ALCOHOL: THE
MORE YOU HAVE OF IT,
THE LESS YOU ARE ABLE
TO SEE ITS EFFECT
ON YOU.

JAY M. BYLSMA

I DISTRUST CAMELS,

AND ANYONE ELSE WHO CAN
GO A WEEK WITHOUT A DRINK.

JOE E. LEWIS

GIMLET

- 60 ml gin
- 15 ml Rose's lime juice
- Slice of lime to garnish

Shake together in a cocktail shaker with ice and strain into a cocktail glass. Garnish with a slice of lime.

The original recipe quantities recorded in The Savoy Cocktail Book are half gin and half Rose's lime juice, but modern tastes have changed and the recipe with them.

A REAL GIMLET IS HALF

AND HALF ROSE'S LIME JUICE AND NOTHING ELSE.

I DON'T KNOW WHAT RECEPTION I'M AT, BUT FOR GOD'S SAKE GIVE ME A GIN AND TONIC.

DENIS THATCHER

NOW IS THE TIME FOR DRINKING,

THE TIME TO DANCE FOOTLOOSE UPON THE EARTH.

HORACE

GIN AND MINT

- 50 ml gin
- two sprigs of fresh mint
- thin slice of cucumber
- 100 ml elderflower pressé
- cucumber or mint to garnish

Stir together the gin, mint and cucumber in a cocktail shaker, making sure you bruise the mint and cucumber.

Strain into a cocktail glass and top with the pressé. Garnish with a sprig of mint or a slice of cucumber.

If you like a little more zing to your summer drink, add a squeeze of lemon juice at the start.

SOBER OR BLOTTO,
THIS IS YOUR MOTTO:
KEEP MUDDLING
THROUGH.

P. G. WODEHOUSE

WHAT HARM IN
DRINKING CAN THERE
BE, SINCE PUNCH AND
LIFE SO WELL AGREE?

THOMAS BLACKLOCK

MAN,
BEING REASONABLE,
MUST GET DRUNK;
THE BEST OF LIFE IS
BUT INTOXICATION.

LORD BYRON

MEDIUM MARTINI

- 20 ml dry vermouth
- 20 ml sweet vermouth
- 40 ml dry gin
- orange or lemon twist to garnish

Shake well in a cooled cocktail shaker and strain into a Martini glass. Serve with either a twist of lemon or orange.

Harry Craddock was the head bartender at the Savoy's American Bar and is credited with popularising the Martini. He wrote the recipe, and over seven hundred others in his greatest work, The Savoy Cocktail Book.

A PERFECT MARTINI SHOULD BE MADE BY FILLING A GLASS WITH GIN THEN WAVING IT IN THE GENERAL DIRECTION OF ITALY.

NOËL COWARD

LET THE GOOD TIMES BEGIN.

RED MEAT

AND GIN.

JULIA CHILD ON HER LONGEVITY

DRINK IS THE FEAST OF REASON AND THE FLOW OF SOUL.

ALEXANDER POPE

ENGLISH GARDEN

- 25ml gin
- 50 ml freshly squeezed apple juice
- 20 ml lime juice
- 20 ml sugar syrup
- sprig of mint
- slice of cucumber, plus extra to garnish

Fill a cocktail shaker with ice and add the gin, apple juice, lime juice and syrup.

Bruise in the mint and cucumber and strain into a Collins glass. Serve with a slice of cucumber.

This is a modern cocktail, reportedly invented in London in 2001, in a collaboration between bartenders Daniel Warner and Tobias Blazquez-Garcia.

DRINK BECAUSE YOU ARE
HAPPY, BUT NEVER BECAUSE
YOU ARE MISERABLE.

G. K. CHESTERTON

GIN ISN'T REALLY A DRINK, IT'S MORE A MASCARA THINNER.

DYLAN MORAN

NINETY-NINE

PER CENT OF ALL PROBLEMS CAN
BE SOLVED BY MONEY – AND
FOR THE OTHER ONE PER CENT
THERE'S ALCOHOL.

QUENTIN R. BUFOGLE

NEGRONI

- 30 ml gin
- 30 ml Campari
- 30 ml sweet vermouth
- orange peel to garnish

Fill an old-fashioned glass halfway to the brim with ice.

Pour the ingredients over the ice and stir. Garnish with the orange peel.

The Negroni is reportedly named after an Italian, Count Negroni. He asked for the classic cocktail, the Americano, to be served with gin instead of soda water and the Negroni was born.

IT TAKES ONLY ONE DRINK TO GET ME DRUNK. THE TROUBLE IS, I CAN'T REMEMBER IF IT'S THE THIRTEENTH OR THE FOURTEENTH.

GEORGE BURNS

ABSTAINER: A WEAK
PERSON WHO YIELDS
TO THE TEMPTATION OF
DENYING HIMSELF
A PLEASURE.

AMBROSE BIERCE

GIN AND
DRUGS,
DEAR LADY,
 G I N
AND DRUGS.

T. S. ELIOT
ON HIS INSPIRATION

FRENCH 75

- 30 ml gin
- 15 ml freshly squeezed lemon juice
- 1 tsp icing sugar
- champagne to finish
- lemon twist to garnish

Mix the gin, lemon juice and sugar together.

Pour into a champagne flute containing cracked ice and fill to the top with champagne. Garnish with a twist of lemon.

Invented in Paris, the kick of the alcohol was said to have felt like being shelled by the French 75 mm field gun used in World War One.

I FEEL WONDERFUL
AND SAD. IT'S
THE GIN.

STEPHEN BERESFORD

DRINK NOT

THE THIRD GLASS, WHICH THOU
CANST NOT TAME, WHEN ONCE
IT IS WITHIN THEE.

GEORGE HERBERT

SIMPLY ENJOY LIFE AND THE GREAT PLEASURES THAT COME WITH IT.

KAROLINA KURKOVA

TOM COLLINS

- 45 ml gin
- 30 ml freshly squeezed lemon juice
- 15 ml sugar syrup
- soda water to finish
- lemon slice and maraschino cherry to garnish

Fill a highball or Collins glass nearly to the brim with ice.

Mix the gin, lemon juice and sugar water together.

Top up with soda water and garnish with a slice of lemon and a maraschino cherry on a cocktail stick.

The first written instance of this classic cocktail appeared in 1876, in a book by famous American mixologist, Jerry Thomas.

A MAN
MUST DEFEND
HIS HOME,
HIS WIFE,
HIS CHILDREN,
AND HIS
MARTINI.

JACKIE GLEASON

I BLOOdy LOVE GIN.

TOO MUCH WORK AND NO
VACATION, DESERVES
AT LEAST A SMALL
LIBATION.

OSCAR WILDE

COME, LANDLORD, FILL A FLOWING BOWL UNTIL IT DOES RUN OVER; TONIGHT WE WILL ALL MERRY BE — TOMORROW WE'LL GET SOBER.

JOHN FLETCHER

PINK GIN

- Three dashes bitters
- 60 ml gin
- Lemon twist to garnish

Add the bitters to an old-fashioned glass and swirl to coat the inside. Drain off any excess liquid.

Pour in the gin and garnish with a lemon twist.

This classic cocktail features strongly in pop culture; even James Bond orders one in the 1965 novel The Man With the Golden Gun.

NO POEMS

CAN LIVE LONG OR PLEASE THAT
ARE WRITTEN BY WATER-DRINKERS.

HORACE

SOBRIETY DIMINISHES,
DISCRIMINATES AND SAYS NO;
DRUNKENNESS EXPANDS,
UNITES AND SAYS YES.

WILLIAM JAMES

WHEN A MAN
WHO IS DRINKING
NEAT

STARTS TALKING
ABOUT HIS MOTHER
HE IS PAST
ALL ARGUMENT.

C. S. FORESTER

BEE'S KNEES

- 50 ml gin
- 10 ml runny honey
- 5 ml water
- 15 ml freshly squeezed lemon juice
- lemon twist to garnish

Stir the honey into the water until blended.

Pour into a cooled cocktail glass and mix in the gin and lemon juice. Serve with a lemon twist.

The rumour is that this Prohibition-era cocktail was flavoured with lemon and honey to hide the taste of the bathtub gin it was made from!

ALCOHOL MAY BE
MAN'S WORST ENEMY,
BUT THE BIBLE SAYS
LOVE YOUR ENEMY.

FRANK SINATRA

TEETOTALLERS LACK THE SYMPATHY AND GENEROSITY OF MEN THAT DRINK.

W. H. DAVIES

NO ANIMAL EVER INVENTED
ANYTHING SO BAD AS
DRUNKENNESS — OR SO
GOOD AS DRINK.

G. K. CHESTERTON

SINGAPORE SLING

- 30 ml gin
- 15 ml cherry liqueur
- 7.5 ml Cointreau
- 7.5 ml DOM Bénédictine
- 10 ml grenadine
- 120 ml freshly squeezed pineapple juice
- 15 ml freshly squeezed lime juice
- dash Angostura bitters
- lemon slice and maraschino cherry to garnish

Add the ingredients to a cocktail shaker full of ice cubes. Shake and strain into a Sling glass and serve with a slice of lemon and a maraschino cherry on a cocktail stick.

The Singapore Sling was famously invented at Raffles Hotel, Singapore.

I WOULD LIKE TO
OBSERVE THE VERMOUTH
FROM ACROSS THE
ROOM WHILE I DRINK
MY MARTINI.

WINSTON CHURCHILL

THE DRINK

YOU LIKE THE BEST SHOULD BE

THE DRINK YOU DRINK

THE MOST.

J. B. BURGESS

A DRINK A  KEEPS THE SHRINK AWAY.

EDWARD ABBEY

VESPER

- 60 ml gin
- 20 ml vodka
- 10 ml Lillet Blanc or Cocchi Americano
- thin strip of lemon

Shake the liquid ingredients together with ice and strain into a Martini glass. Serve with the lemon.

Ian Fleming invented the Vesper, introducing it in the 1953 James Bond novel Casino Royale. *Bond named it after the beautiful Vesper Lynd.*

I NEVER GO JOGGING; IT MAKES ME SPILL MY MARTINI.

GEORGE BURNS

DRINKING IS A WAY OF ENDING THE DAY.

ERNEST HEMINGWAY

WHEN I DRINK
I THINK; AND WHEN
I THINK, I DRINK.

FRANÇOIS RABELAIS

THE CHURCH

IS NEAR, BUT THE ROAD IS ICY.
THE BAR IS FAR, BUT I WILL
WALK CAREFULLY.

RUSSIAN PROVERB

LONG ISLAND ICE TEA

- 15 ml vodka
- 15 ml gin
- 15 ml white rum
- 15 ml tequila
- 15 ml triple sec
- 30 ml freshly squeezed lemon juice
- 30 ml gomme syrup
- splash cola
- lemon twist or wedge to garnish

Fill a highball glass halfway to the brim with ice.

Pour the ingredients over and stir. Serve with a twist or wedge of lemon.

This drink's origins are hotly contested; many claim it was invented by Old Man Bishop during the Prohibition era.

A MAN'S GOT TO BELIEVE IN SOMETHING. I BELIEVE I'LL HAVE ANOTHER DRINK.

W. C. FIELDS

THE PROPER UNION

OF GIN AND VERMOUTH IS A
GREAT AND SUDDEN GLORY;
IT IS ONE OF THE HAPPIEST
MARRIAGES ON EARTH, AND
ONE OF THE SHORTEST LIVED.

BERNARD DeVOTO

KEEPING
ONE'S GUESTS
SUPPLIED WITH
LIQUOR IS THE
FIRST

OF HOSPITALITY.

MARGARET WAY

PINK LADY

- 45 ml gin
- one egg white
- four dashes grenadine
- maraschino cherry to garnish

Fill a cocktail shaker with ice and shake together the ingredients.

Strain into a cocktail glass and serve with maraschino cherry.

Said to be the favourite cocktail of pink-fanatic screen siren Jayne Mansfield, who reportedly drank one before every meal.

WOMAN FIRST TEMPTED MAN TO EAT; HE TOOK TO DRINKING OF HIS OWN ACCORD.

JOHN R. KEMBLE

REALITY IS AN ILLUSION CREATED BY A LACK OF ALCOHOL.

N. F. SIMPSON

BUT I'M NOT SO THINK AS YOU DRUNK I AM.

J. C. SQUIRE

DRY MARTINI

- 30 ml dry vermouth
- 60 ml dry gin
- dash orange bitters
- orange or lemon twist to garnish

Shake well in a cooled cocktail shaker and strain into a Martini glass and serve with a twist of orange or lemon.

Hemingway preferred a 'Montgomery' dry Martini – 15 parts gin to one part vermouth. The Montgomery was named after a general who would only attack when his army outnumbered the enemy's at least 15 to 1.

A MAN OUGHT TO GET
DRUNK AT LEAST TWICE
A YEAR... SO HE WON'T
LET HIMSELF GET
SNOTTY ABOUT IT.

RAYMOND CHANDLER

THE PROBLEM

WITH THE WORLD IS THAT
EVERYONE IS A FEW
DRINKS BEHIND.

HUMPHREY BOGART

WHEN I'M DRUNK, I

BETTE MIDLER

GIN AND TONIC

- 30 ml gin
- 90 ml tonic
- garnish to taste

Put several ice cubes into a highball or cabernet glass and pour over the ingredients.

Which garnish you use will depend on the flavour you are trying to enhance: for dry gin try lime or an olive; for floral gins try grapefruit, rosemary or cucumber; for citrussy or spiced gins add coriander or orange.

WHAT'S DRINKING? A MERE PAUSE FROM THINKING!

LORD BYRON

TURN IMPOSSIBLE INTO GINPOSSIBLE!

BELOVED,

WE JOIN HANDS HERE TO PRAY
FOR GIN... OUR INNARDS THIRST
FOR THE JUICE OF JUNIPER.

WALLACE THURMAN

HERE'S TO ALCOHOL,
THE ROSE-COLOURED
GLASSES OF
LIFE.

F. SCOTT FITZGERALD

THE LAST WORD

- 30 ml gin
- 20 ml green chartreuse
- 20 ml maraschino liqueur
- 20 ml freshly squeezed lime juice
- lime wedge or maraschino cherry to garnish

Fill a cocktail shaker with ice and add the ingredients. Add a splash of chilled water to taste if necessary.

Shake together then strain into a Martini or coupe glass. Serve with a wedge of lime or a maraschino cherry.

When The Last Word first appeared on the Detroit Athletic Club's menu in 1916, it cost 35 cents and it was the club's most expensive drink.

I HAD NEVER TASTED ANYTHING SO COOL AND CLEAN.

ERNEST HEMINGWAY
ON MARTINIS

YOU'RE NOT DRUNK IF
YOU CAN LIE ON THE
FLOOR WITHOUT
HOLDING
ON.

DEAN MARTIN

HAPPINESS IS... FINDING TWO OLIVES IN YOUR MARTINI WHEN YOU'RE HUNGRY.

JOHNNY CARSON

PEGU CLUB

- 60 ml gin
- 30 ml orange liqueur
- 20 ml freshly squeezed lime juice
- dash orange bitters
- slice of lime

Combine all the liquid ingredients in a shaker, add ice and shake well.

Strain into a cocktail glass and serve with a slice of lime.

This cocktail was the signature drink of Burma's Pegu Club, the social centre for colonial Britons in the 1920s.

NOTHING

IS MORE PLEASURABLE THAN
TO SIT IN THE SHADE, SIP GIN
AND CONTEMPLATE OTHER
PEOPLE'S ADULTERIES.

JOHN SKOW

SOMETIMES TOO
MUCH TO DRINK IS
BARELY ENOUGH.

MARK TWAIN

I DRINK WHEN I HAVE OCCASION, AND SOMETIMES WHEN I HAVE NO OCCASION.

MIGUEL de CERVANTES

CLOVER CLUB

- 40 ml gin
- 10 ml sweet vermouth
- handful fresh raspberries
- 10 ml freshly squeezed lemon juice
- 2 tsp raspberry syrup
- one egg white
- lemon twist or raspberry to garnish

Combine and shake all the ingredients vigorously for 10 seconds, then add ice and shake for another 10 seconds.

Strain into a cocktail or coupe glass and serve with a lemon twist or a raspberry.

The Clover Club is named after a nineteenth-century Philadelphia men's club.

NEVER TRUST A MAN
WHO DOESN'T
DRINK.

JAMES CRUMLEY

THE THREE-MARTINI

LUNCH IS THE EPITOME OF
AMERICAN EFFICIENCY. WHERE
ELSE CAN YOU GET AN EARFUL,
A BELLYFUL AND A SNOOTFUL
AT THE SAME TIME?

GERALD FORD

THE WORSE YOU ARE AT THINKING, THE BETTER YOU ARE AT DRINKING.

TERRY GOODKIND

GIBSON

- 70 ml gin
- dash dry vermouth
- 2 cocktail onions

Pour the ingredients into an ice-filled shaker and stir for 5–10 seconds.

Strain into a Martini glass and garnish with two cocktail onions.

The Gibson featured in Hitchcock's North by Northwest when Cary Grant's impeccably dressed Roger Thornhill orders one during a seductive dinner on a train.

I AM PREPARED TO BELIEVE THAT A DRY MARTINI SLIGHTLY IMPAIRS THE PALATE, BUT THINK WHAT IT DOES FOR THE SOUL.

ALEC WAUGH

I HAVE TAKEN MORE
OUT OF ALCOHOL THAN
ALCOHOL HAS TAKEN
OUT OF ME.

WINSTON CHURCHILL

DRINK

WHAT YOU WANT;
DRINK WHAT YOU'RE ABLE.
IF YOU ARE DRINKING
WITH ME, YOU'LL
BE UNDER THE TABLE.

ANONYMOUS

THE MOLL

- 30 ml sloe gin
- 30 ml gin
- 30 ml dry vermouth
- dash orange bitters
- 1 tsp sugar

Shake the ingredients over ice in a shaker.

Strain into a chilled cocktail glass.

The Moll is named after Daniel Defoe's enterprising heroine, Moll Flanders.

AH, DRINK AGAIN THIS RIVER THAT IS THE TAKER-AWAY OF P A I N, AND THE GIVER-BACK OF BEAUTY!

EDNA ST VINCENT MILLAY

HE WAS WHITE AND SHAKEN, LIKE A Ⓓ Ⓡ Ⓨ MARTINI.

P. G. WODEHOUSE

ALWAYS

DO SOBER WHAT YOU SAID
YOU'D DO DRUNK. THAT WILL
TEACH YOU TO KEEP YOUR
MOUTH SHUT.

ERNEST HEMINGWAY

RIVIERA SNOB

- 60 ml Aperol
- 30 ml gin
- 20 ml lemon juice
- 15 ml sugar syrup
- soda to finish
- orange peel to garnish

Combine ingredients in a chilled cocktail shaker and shake well, until cooled.

Strain into a coupe glass and garnish with a twist of orange peel.

Aperol was invented by the Barbieri brothers in 1919 and marketed specifically at women because of its low alcohol content.

MARTINIS ARE THE ONLY
AMERICAN INVENTION
AS PERFECT AS
THE SONNET.

H. L. MENCKEN

WITH ENOUGH GIN I COULD DO ANYTHING.

HEALTH —
WHAT MY
FRIENDS
ARE ALWAYS
DRINKING TO
BEFORE THEY
FALL DOWN.

PHYLLIS DILLER

YOU HAVE TO
DRINK, OTHERWISE
YOU'D GO STARK
STARING SOBER.

KEITH WATERHOUSE

LAVENDER AND GIN

- 50 ml lavender gin (see below)
- 100 ml lemonade dash
- freshly squeezed lemon juice
- lavender stalk to garnish

To make the lavender gin, add 20 dried lavender flower heads to a 70 cl bottle of gin and leave overnight to infuse, then remove the lavender.

Add the gin to an ice-filled highball glass and top up with the lemonade. Add a dash of lemon juice and stir.

Garnish with a lavender stalk.

The lavender taste gives a traditional English summertime feel to the cocktail.

TIME IS NEVER WASTED WHEN YOU'RE WASTED ALL THE TIME.

CATHERINE ZANDONELLA

DRUNKENNESS IS NOTHING BUT VOLUNTARY MADNESS.

SENECA THE YOUNGER

I FEAR THE MAN WHO
DRINKS WATER AND
SO REMEMBERS THIS
MORNING WHAT THE
REST OF US SAID
LAST NIGHT.

ANONYMOUS

MONKEY GLAND

- 60 ml gin
- 40 ml freshly squeezed orange juice
- 1 tsp grenadine
- 1 tsp sugar syrup
- 1 tsp absinthe
- orange twist to garnish

Put the ingredients into a shaker with ice and shake well.

Strain into a cocktail glass and garnish with a twist of orange.

This cocktail is named after the unsavoury historical practice of grafting a monkey testicle to a human in the belief that it would make one live longer.

A MAN CAN HIDE ALL THINGS, EXCEPTING TWAIN — THAT HE IS DRUNK, AND THAT HE IS IN LOVE.

ANTIPHANES

GIN MAKES THE WORLD GO ROUND.

I NEVER MET A PUB
I DIDN'T LIKE.

PETE SLOSBERG

ALCOHOL

MAY NOT SOLVE YOUR
PROBLEMS, BUT NEITHER
WILL WATER OR MILK.

ANONYMOUS

LONDON FOG

- 40 ml gin
- 20 ml Pernod
- orange twist to garnish

Fill an old-fashioned glass with crushed ice and add the ingredients.

Stir well, adding more ice if necessary and an orange twist to garnish.

The cocktail gained this name thanks to its murky green colour: it is a similar hue to the 'pea-soup' fog that pervaded London until the twentieth century.

I ENVY PEOPLE WHO DRINK —
AT LEAST THEY KNOW WHAT
TO BLAME EVERYTHING ON.

OSCAR LEVANT

I NEVER DRINK WHILE I'M WORKING, BUT AFTER A FEW GLASSES I GET IDEAS THAT WOULD NEVER HAVE OCCURRED TO ME DEAD SOBER.

IRWIN SHAW

THE DRUNK MIND

SPEAKS THE SOBER HEART.

ANONYMOUS

CAMOMILE AND GIN

- 60 ml gin
- 25 ml camomile tea
- 25 ml pink grapefruit or lemon juice
- 15 ml honey
- lime twist to garnish

Shake the ingredients vigorously in a shaker until mixed.

Strain into a coupe glass and garnish with a twist of lime.

Camomile is said to have many health benefits: it can be used to treat anything from hay fever to chicken pox!

I DRINK EXACTLY
AS MUCH AS
I WANT, AND
O N E
DRINK MORE.

H. L. MENCKEN

A GIN A DAY KEEPS THE DOCTOR AWAY.

ALCOHOL

IS A MISUNDERSTOOD VITAMIN.

P. G. WODEHOUSE

I HAVE A THEORY
THAT THE SECRET OF
MARITAL HAPPINESS
IS SIMPLE: DRINK IN
DIFFERENT PUBS TO
YOUR OTHER HALF.

JILLY COOPER

AVIATION

- 60 ml gin
- 15 ml maraschino liqueur
- 10 ml crème de violette
- 20 ml freshly squeezed lemon juice
- cherry or lemon twist to garnish

Combine all the liquid ingredients in a shaker, add ice and shake well until mixed.

Strain into a chilled cocktail glass and serve with a cherry or a twist of lemon.

If the crème de violette proves difficult to find, a variation in The Savoy Cocktail Book allows it to be omitted, although the drink will lose its distinctive lavender colour.

THE ONLY CURE FOR
A REAL HANGOVER
IS DEATH.

ROBERT BENCHLEY

HOW MUCH OF OUR LITERATURE, OUR POLITICAL LIFE, OUR FRIENDSHIPS AND LOVE AFFAIRS, DEPEND ON BEING ABLE TO TALK PEACEFULLY IN A BAR!

JOHN WAIN

THERE IS NOTHING

WHICH HAS YET BEEN CONTRIVED
BY MAN, BY WHICH SO MUCH
HAPPINESS IS PRODUCED AS BY
A GOOD TAVERN OR INN.

SAMUEL JOHNSON

OLD ETONIAN

- 40 ml gin
- 40 ml Lillet Blanc or Cocchi Americano
- dash crème de Noyaux
- dash orange bitters
- orange twist to garnish

Add the ingredients to a shaker filled with ice and shake.

Strain into a cocktail glass and garnish with a twist of orange.

The Old Etonian enjoyed its heyday in the mid 1920s, when it was quaffed around London, home of Eton College.

ALCOHOL IS LIKE
LOVE. THE FIRST KISS
IS MAGIC, THE SECOND
IS INTIMATE, THE THIRD
IS ROUTINE.

RAYMOND CHANDLER

WHY BE SOBER WHEN YOU CAN HAVE GIN?

ALCOHOL IS THE ANAESTHESIA BY WHICH WE ENDURE THE OPERATION OF .

GEORGE BERNARD SHAW

ALCOHOL

IS NECESSARY FOR A MAN
SO THAT HE CAN HAVE A
GOOD OPINION OF HIMSELF,
UNDISTURBED BY THE FACTS.

FINLEY PETER DUNNE

SLOE GIN FIZZ

- 60 ml sloe gin
- 30 ml freshly squeezed lemon or lime juice
- 1 tsp sugar syrup
- 115 ml soda water
- slice of lemon to garnish

Shake the gin, lemon juice and sugar syrup over ice in a shaker.

Strain into an ice-filled highball or Sling glass. Top up with the soda water and stir. Garnish with a slice of lemon.

Sloe gin is so popular in the UK that there are several competitions and awards, including the Sloe Gin World Championships in East Sussex.

BACCHUS: A CONVENIENT DEITY INVENTED BY THE ANCIENTS AS AN EXCUSE FOR GETTING DRUNK.

AMBROSE BIERCE

KNOW THYSELF,
ESPECIALLY THYSELF
AFTER A COUPLE
OF DRINKS.

ROBERT BRAULT

THE WORST THING

ABOUT SOME MEN IS THAT

WHEN THEY ARE NOT DRUNK

THEY ARE SOBER.

W. B. YEATS

FIFTY-FIFTY MARTINI

- 40 ml gin
- 40 ml dry vermouth
- two dashes orange bitters (optional)
- olive to garnish

Combine the ingredients and ice in a shaker and stir for 20 seconds.

Strain into a Martini glass and garnish with an olive.

Also known as a 'Perfect Martini', this is likely the mix the Martini started life as before evolving into the more bracing drink of today.

THE GIN AND TONIC HAS
SAVED MORE ENGLISHMEN'S
LIVES AND MINDS, THAN ALL
THE DOCTORS IN THE EMPIRE.

WINSTON CHURCHILL

SOUP OF THE DAY: GIN.

MY GRANDMOTHER IS OVER 80 AND STILL DOESN'T NEED GLASSES. DRINKS RIGHT OUT OF THE BOTTLE.

HENNY YOUNGMAN

DRINK THE FIRST.

THE SECOND SLOWLY. SKIP THE THIRD.

KNUTE ROCKNE

MAE ROSE

- 40 ml gin
- 20 ml dry vermouth
- 12.5 ml Campari
- 12.5 ml grapefruit liqueur
- grapefruit twist to garnish

Put the ingredients and ice into a shaker and stir until the shaker is cold on the outside.

Strain into a champagne coupe and serve with a twist of grapefruit.

You'll need to put extra time into cooling this cocktail as it should be served very cold.

ONE

MORE DRINK AND I'D HAVE BEEN UNDER THE HOST!

DOROTHY PARKER

GIN AND BEAR IT.

If you're interested in finding out more about our books, find us on Facebook at **Summersdale Publishers** and follow us on Twitter at @Summersdale.

www.summersdale.com